90 Days of Self-Gratitude for the Overworked Dental Hygienist

Copyright © 2020 by Melissa Rosochacki

All rights reserved. No part of this book may be reproduced or used in any manner without written permission of the copyright owner.

Published by Evard Publishing

www.evardpublishing.com

www.brilliancemaven.com

Introduction:

Those of us as dental professionals are not exempt or immune from feelings of despair. We have those days where we just can't seem to get it right. We fall under the desire to do it all perfectly. What I stand by and I know to be true is that we can not attain perfection. It's important for each one of us just to ensure we are doing all that we can to be the best versions of ourselves on any given day.

This journal is designed to allow you, the reader, the opportunity to perform a little bit of self reflection to ensure that you are not only seeing the wonderfulness that truly does still abound in this world, but also all of the brilliance that exists within you. This is worthy of repeating, without a doubt each and every one of you that holds this book has a brilliance within. This journal is just one of many tools that will aid you in not forgetting this profound fact.

How to Use this Journal:

This is a guided journal. It is designed with thought provoking prompts to help you dive deep and keep you reminded of all those things that you can display gratitude for. It gives you an opportunity to reflect on what experiences you have as part of your career in the dental field as well as some opportunities for personal reflection.

This journal is very personal and is designed to be individualized by you the reader. You can follow the journal along in chronological order if that is what suits you best. Another option is to skip through the book and answer the prompts that seem the most appropriate for you that day. With either option, the goal is that you will take the time daily as part of your night time routine to complete the prompts and finish this journal within 90 days.

Once the journal is completed, it will be very appropriate to schedule some time to fully reflect upon the things that you have learned about yourself and the best way to navigate in the professional space to continue to find areas of gratitude and continuously develop. Some may choose to complete a second guide and see how they have grown from the first. Others will dive a little deeper and follow through with other books offered in the series to continue on the satisfying path of self discovery.

My wish for you is that you love this journal and are able to begin to truly understand your brilliance in the process.

Your Cheerleader in Dentistry,
Melissa Rosochacki, MBA, RDH, CDA

This Journal Belongs to:

....

Love Your Sister in Hygiene

Melissa Rose

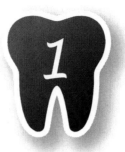

What's something that you're looking forward to?

What's a simple pleasure that you're grateful for?

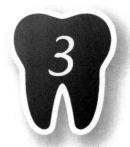

What's something that you are grateful to have today that you didn't have a year ago?

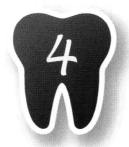

What's something about your body or health that you're grateful for?

What's an accomplishment you're proud of?

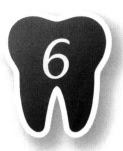

What's a possession that makes your life easier?

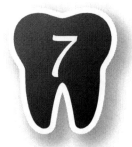

Open your phone and find a photo that you like. Why are you grateful for this photo? What are you grateful for in the photo?

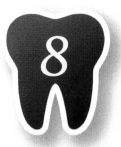

What have you been given that you're grateful for?

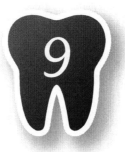

What's something or someone that makes you feel safe?

What do you like about your career choice?

How are you able to help others outside of work?

Write about a friend that you're grateful for.

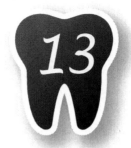

Write about a family member that you're grateful for.

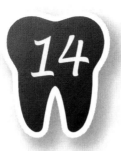

What did you accomplish today?

What's a tradition that you're grateful for?

What's one of your personality traits that you're grateful for?

What mistake or failure are you grateful for?

What skill(s) do you have that you're grateful for?

What's something that you bought recently that you're grateful for?

Write about 3 things you're grateful for today.

What is something that you have created that you are really proud of?

What did you do to make someone smile today?

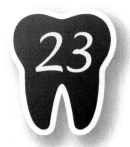

What is something beautiful that you saw today?

What is something that was hard to do but you did it anyway?

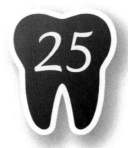

What is a trial or challenge that strengthened you?

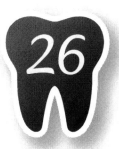

What did you learn about yourself today?

Who made you feel important today?

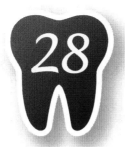

What is something that relaxes you after a long day?

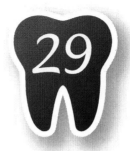

Write about a recent small success?

What is a CE topic that you are so thankful to have been able to refresh your memory about?

Who is someone that inspires you to be great?

Write a thank you note to someone that made your week easier.

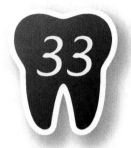

Write about the most inspiring mentor during your career.

Write about a favorite quote or saying that just makes you happy.

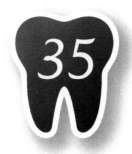

What foods are you most grateful for?

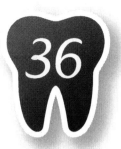

What are the ways you show gratitude to others?

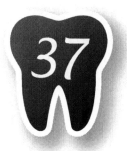

What are the ways you show gratitude to yourself?

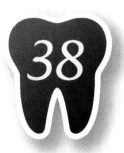

What are the ways you would like other people to show gratitude to you?

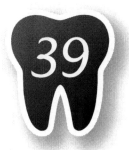

What memory from dental school are you most grateful for?

What opportunities are you grateful for?

Write about something that has been a wish come true in your life.

What is one thing that you can share with someone hoping to follow in your footsteps personally?

Reflect on the start of your dental career and today. What 3 things are you most grateful for?

What patient interaction were you most grateful for this week?

What information would you share with a complete stranger to give them some insight into who you are?

Write about your ideal day in the dental office and what you do daily in an effort to achieve it.

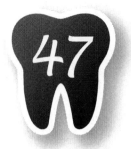

Write about the most inspiring mentor during school.

Write the lyrics from a song that inspires you and the reason why.

Take this time to write a note to yourself 10 years from now, what things do you expect will have changed?

What are some positive habits that you are grateful for?

What was the most unusual compliment you ever received?

What is the most unique way that a patient expressed their gratefulness to you?

Who is the last person to tell you that you are appreciated? Write about that experience.

What things are you taking for granted day to day that you need to pause and be grateful for?

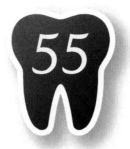

What is your proudest accomplishment related to your career?

What person is in your life that is bringing something positive that you didn't have a year ago?

What risk are you most grateful for having taken?

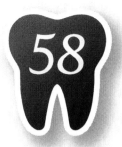

What goal have you recently achieved that has had a great impact on your life?

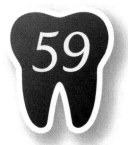

Where have you recently discovered unexpected beauty?

Write about something you are looking forward to within the next 6 months.

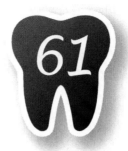

Described the last time you "helped" someone

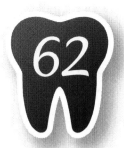

What advice do you need to give yourself today?

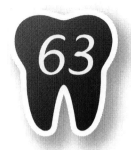

What is one thing that you can share with someone hoping to follow in your footsteps professionally?

If you could relive one moment in your career, which would it be and why?

What moment most changed your career for the best?

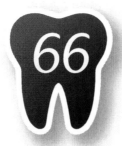

What is one thing you look forward to after work each day?

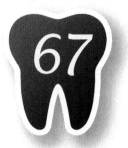

Write about a teacher or mentor that you're grateful for.

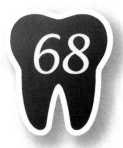

What thing makes you feel the most successful/accomplished?

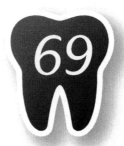

What quote made you think about your career differently?

Think of something good you did for yourself recently and write yourself a thank you note.

Write a letter to someone that you need to forgive.

Who is someone you find it difficult to get along with. Write at least 3 positive qualities they have.

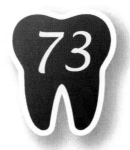

Write about something you are naturally talented at.

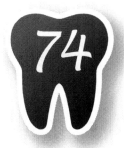

Write about the one person that stands by you through all times, good and bad.

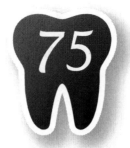

What are three ways you can say thank you without using the words thank you (no you can't just say thank you in another language...lol)?

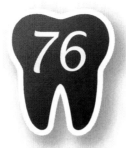

If you had to give up all of your possessions with the exception of 3 things, what would they be?

Who were you able to comfort this week? Describe how

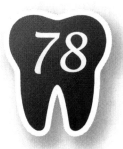

What insight did you gain today?

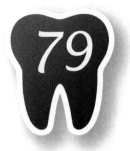

How did you show yourself compassion today?

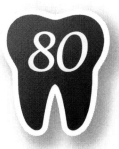

What problem were you able to resolve today?

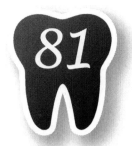

Reflect on this current season, what excites you about this time of year?

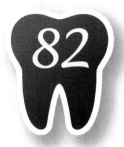

What clothing makes you feel confident and why?

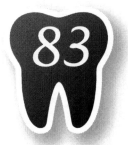

Describe your perfect vacation, get very detailed.

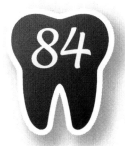

What career advancements are you longing for? What are you doing to reach them?

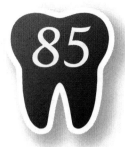

What was the last thing that you did even though you were afraid?

How do you show gratitude to your patients?

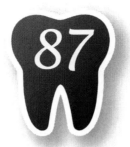

Write a thank you note to someone that influenced you to join this profession.

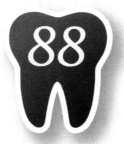

What do you enjoy most about the room you are currently in?

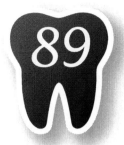

What is the most adrenaline producing thing you have done? What made you do it?

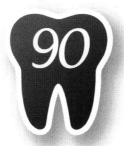

If you were to teach a master class, what would the topic be?

Made in the USA
Middletown, DE
10 September 2020